Contents

INTRODUCTION

The fantasy that a machine is capable of simulating the human visual system is old. We've come a long way since the first university papers appeared back in the 1960s, as evidenced by the advent of modern systems trivially integrated into mobile applications.

Today, computer vision is one of the hottest subfields of artificial intelligence and machine learning, given its wide variety of applications and tremendous potential. Its goal: to replicate the powerful capacities of human vision.

But what exactly is computer vision? How is it currently applied in different industries? What are some well-known business use cases? What tasks are typical to computer vision?

In this guide, you'll learn about the basic concept of computer vision and how it's used in the real world. It's a simple examination of a complex problem for anybody who has ever heard of computer vision but isn't quite sure what it's all about and how it's applied.

Feel free to read through the guide in its entirety or jump directly to one of the sections below.

Let's get started.

What is computer vision?

The problem it solves

As humans, we are capable of understanding and describing a scene encapsulated in an image. This involves much more than detecting four people in the foreground, one street, and several cars as in the image below.

Aside from that basic information, we are able to understand that the people in the foreground are walking, that one of them is barefoot — a curious thing — and we even know who they are. We can reasonably infer that they are not in danger of being hit by a car and that the white Volkswagen is poorly parked. A human would also have no problem describing the clothes they are wearing and, in addition to indicating the color, guessing at the material and texture of each outfit.

These are also the skills a computer vision system needs. In a few words, the main problem solved by computer vision can be summarized as follows:

Given a two-dimensional image, a computer vision system must recognize the present objects and their characteristics such as shapes, textures, colors, sizes, spatial arrangement, among other things, to provide a description as complete as possible of the image.

Distinguishing computer vision from related fields

It is important to understand that computer vision accomplishes much more than other fields such as image processing or machine vision, with which it shares several characteristics. Let's have a look at the differences between the fields.

Image processing

Image processing is focused on processing raw images to apply some kind of transformation. Usually, the goal is to improve images or prepare them as an input for a specific task, while in computer vision the goal is to describe and explain images. For instance, noise reduction, contrast, or rotation operations, typical components of image processing, can be performed at pixel level and do not need a complex grasp of the image that allows for some understanding of what is happening in it.

Machine vision

This is a particular case where computer vision is used to perform some actions, typically in production or manufacturing lines. In the chemical industry, machine vision systems can help with the manufacturing of products by checking the containers in the line (are they clean, empty, and free of damage?) or by checking that the final product is properly sealed.

Computer vision

Computer vision can solve more complex problems such as facial recognition (used, for example, by Snapchat to apply filters), detailed image analysis that allows for visual searches like the ones Google Images performs, or biometric identification methods.

Industry applications

Humans are not only capable of understanding scenes corresponding to images, but also of interpreting handwriting, impressionist or abstract paintings and, with a little training, the 2D ultrasound of a baby.

In that sense, the field of computer vision is particularly complex, possessing an immense range of practical applications.

The good thing about innovation that relies on artificial Intelligence and machine learning, in general, and computer vision, in particular, is that companies of all types and sizes, from the e-commerce industry to more classic ones, can take advantage of its powerful capabilities.

Let's take a look at some of the industry applications that have been the most impactful in recent years.

Retail

The use of computer vision in the retail sector has been one of the most important technological trends in recent years. Below, you'll be introduced to some very common use cases.

Behavioral tracking

Brick and mortar retailer's use computer vision algorithms in combination with store cameras to understand who their customers are and how they behave.

Algorithms are able to recognize faces and determine human characteristics, such as gender or age range. What's more, retailer's can use computer vision techniques to track customers' movements through stores, analyze navigational routes, detect walking patterns, and measure storefront attention times, as showed in this demo:

Adding directional gaze detection, retailers are able to answer a crucial question: where to put the items in the store to improve the consumer experience and maximize sales.

Computer vision is also an excellent tool for developing anti-theft mechanisms. Among other things, face recognition algorithms can be trained to spot known shoplifters or to detect when someone is hiding an item in their backpack.

Inventory management

When it comes to inventory management, there are two main computer vision applications.

Through security camera image analysis, a computer vision algorithm can generate a very accurate estimate of the items available in the store. This is extremely valuable information for store managers, who can immediately become aware of an unusual increase in demand and react early and efficiently.

Another fairly common application is analyzing the use of shelf space to identify suboptimal configurations. In addition to discovering lost space, an algorithm of this nature can suggest better item placement.

Manufacturing

Major problems that can occur on a manufacturing line are the breaking of machines or the production of defective components. These result in delays and significant losses in profits.

Computer vision algorithms prove to be a great means of predictive maintenance. By analyzing visual information (e.g., from cameras attached to robots), algorithms can identify potential trouble before it occurs. The fact that a system can anticipate that a packaging or car assembly robot will fail is a huge contribution.

The same idea applies to defect reduction, where the system can spot defects in components throughout the entire production line. This allows manufacturer's to take action in real time and decide what should be done to resolve the issue. Perhaps the defect is not so serious and the process can continue, but the product is flagged in some way or redirected through a specific production path. Sometimes, however, it may be necessary to stop the production line. Of further interest is that the system can be trained, for each use case, to classify the defects by types and degrees of severity.

Healthcare

In the healthcare domain, the number of existing computer vision applications is impressive.

Undoubtedly, medical image analysis is the best-known example, since it helps to significantly improve the medical diagnostic process. Images from MRIs, CT scans, and X-rays are analyzed to find anomalies such as tumors or search for signs of neurological illnesses.

In many cases, it's all about image analysis techniques, which extract features from images in order to train a classifier to be able to detect anomalies. However, there are specific applications where finer processing is required. For example, in the analysis of images from colonoscopies, it is necessary to segment the images to look for polyps and prevent colorectal cancer.

The image above is a result of image segmentation used to visualize thoracic elements. The system segments and colors each important part: the pulmonary arteries (blue), the pulmonary veins (red), the mediastinum (yellow), and the diaphragm (violet).

A large amount of applications of this type are currently in use, as varied as techniques that estimate the amount of blood lost due to postpartum hemorrhages; quantify coronary artery calcium; and evaluate blood flow in the human body without an MRI.

But medical imaging is not the only area where computer vision can play an important role. For instance, with respect to visually impaired people, there are setups that assist them to navigate indoor environments safely. These systems can place the person and the surrounding objects in a floor plan, among other things, to provide a visual experience in real time. Gaze tracking and eye area analysis can be used to detect early cognitive impairments such as autism or dyslexia in children, which are highly correlated with unusual gaze behavior.

Autonomous vehicles

Have you ever wondered how self-driving cars can "see"? The field of computer vision plays a central role in the domain of autonomous vehicles, since it allows them to perceive and understand the environment around them in order to operate correctly.

One of the most exciting challenges in computer vision is object detection in images and videos. This involves locating a varying number of objects and the ability to classify them, in order to distinguish if an object is a traffic light, a car, or a person, as in the video below.

This kind of technology, combined with the analysis of data from other sources, such as sensors and/or radars, is what allows a car to "see".

Object detection in images is a complex and powerful task that we have discussed in depth in the article, Object Detection with Deep Learning: The Definitive Guide.

Insurance

The use of computer vision in insurance has had great impact, particularly in claims processing.

A computer vision application can guide clients through the process of visually documenting a claim. In real time, it can analyze images and send them to the appropriate agents. At the same time, it can estimate and adjust repair costs, determine if the insurance covers them and even check for possible fraud. All this minimizes the length of the claims cycle, resulting in a better client experience.

From a preventive point of view, computer vision is of immense help in avoiding accidents; there are applications for preventing collisions, integrated into industrial machinery, cars, and drones. This is a new era of risk management that will most likely change the insurance field.

Agriculture

Agriculture is a major industry where computer vision is having a tremendous impact, especially in the area of precision agriculture.

In grain production, a global economic activity, a series of valuable applications have been developed. Grain production faces certain recurring issues, which historically have been monitored by humans. However, computer vision algorithms can now detect, or in some cases can reasonably predict, diseases or pest and insect infestations. Early diagnosis allows farmers to take appropriate measures quickly, reducing losses and ensuring production quality.

Another permanent challenge is weed control, considering that weeds have become resistant to herbicides over time and represent significant losses for farmers. There are robots with integrated computer vision technology that monitor an entire farm and spray herbicides precisely. This saves huge volumes of pesticides, which is an incredible benefit for the planet and in terms of production costs.

Soil quality is likewise a major factor in agriculture. There are applications that can recognize, from images taken with mobile phones, potential defects and nutritional deficiencies in soils. After analyzing the images sent, these applications suggest soil restoration techniques and possible solutions to the problems detected.

Computer vision can be further used in sorting. There are algorithms for sorting fruits, vegetables, and even flowers, by identifying their main properties (e.g., size, quality, weight, color, texture). These algorithms are additionally capable of spotting defects and estimating which items will last longer and which should be sent to local markets. This leads to the maximization of the shelf-life of the items and reduces time-to-market.

Defense and Security

Similar to the case of retailers, companies with high security requirements, such as banks or casinos, can benefit from computer vision applications that allow them to identify customers based on analyzing images from security cameras.

On another level, computer vision is a powerful ally in terms of homeland security tasks. It can be used to improve cargo inspection at ports or for surveillance of sensitive places such as embassies, power plants, hospitals, railroads, and stadiums. The main idea in this context is that computer vision not only analyzes and classifies images, but can also build detailed and meaningful descriptions of a scene, providing, in real time, key elements for decision-makers.

In general, computer vision is used extensively in defense tasks such as reconnaissance of enemy terrain, automatic identification of enemies in images, automating vehicle and machine movements, and search and rescue.

Typical tasks in computer vision

How is it possible to replicate the human visual system with a high level of precision?

Computer vision is based on an extensive set of diverse tasks, combined to achieve highly sophisticated applications. The most frequent tasks in computer vision are image and video recognition, which basically consist of determining the different objects an image contains.

Image classification

Probably one of the most well-known tasks in computer vision is image classification. It allows for the classification of a given image as belonging to one of a set of predefined categories. Let's take a simple binary example: we want to categorize images according to whether they contain a tourist attraction or not. Suppose that a classifier is built for this purpose and that the image below is provided.

The classifier will respond that the image belongs to the group of images containing tourist attractions. This does not mean that it has necessarily recognized the Eiffel Tower but rather that it has previously seen photos of the tower and that it has been told that those images contain a tourist attraction.

A more ambitious version of the classifier could have more than two categories. For example, there could be a category for each specific type of tourist attraction that we want to recognize: Eiffel Tower, Arc de Triomphe, Sacré-Coeur, etc. In such a scenario, the answers per image input could be multiple, as in the case of the postcard above.

Localization

Suppose now that we not only want to know which tourist attractions appear in an image, but are also interested in knowing exactly where they are. The goal of localization is to find the location of a single object in an image. For example, in the image below, the Eiffel Tower has been localized.

The standard way to perform localization is to define a bounding box enclosing the object in the image.

Localization is a particularly useful task. It can allow for the automatic cropping of objects in a set of images, for instance. If it is combined with the classification task, it could allow us to quickly build a dataset of (cropped) images of famous tourist attractions.

Object detection

If we imagine an action involving simultaneous location and classification, repeated for all objects of interest in an image, we end up with object detection. In this case, the number of objects an image can contain is unknown, if it contains any at all. The purpose of object detection is, therefore, to find and then classify a variable number of objects in an image.

In this particularly dense image, we see how a computer vision system identifies a large number of different objects: cars, people, bicycles, and even street signs containing text.

The problem would be complex even for a human. Some objects are only partially visible, either because they're partly outside the frame or because they are overlapping each other. Also, the size of similar objects vary greatly.

A straightforward application of object detection is counting. The applications in real life are quite diverse, from counting different types of fruit harvested to counting people at events such as public demonstrations or football matches.

Object identification

Object identification is slightly different from object detection, although similar techniques are often used to achieve them both. In this case, given a specific object, the goal is to find instances of said object in images. It is not about classifying an image, as we saw previously, but about determining if the object appears in an image or not, and if it does appear, specifying the location (s) where it appears. An example may be searching for images that contain the logo of a specific company. Another example is monitoring real time images from security cameras to identify a specific person's face.

Instance segmentation

Instance segmentation can be seen as a next step after object detection. In this case, it's not only about finding objects in an image, but also about creating a mask for each detected object that is as accurate as possible.

You can see in the image above how the instance segmentation algorithm finds masks for the four Beatles and some cars (although the result is incomplete, especially where it comes to Lennon).

Such results would be very expensive if the tasks were carried out manually, but the technology makes it easy to achieve them. In France, the law prohibits exposing children in the media without the explicit consent of their parents. Using instance segmentation techniques, it's possible to blur out young children's faces on television or in film, when they are interviewed or captured outdoors, as may be the case during student strikes.

Object tracking

The purpose of object tracking is to track an object that is in motion over time, utilizing consecutive video frames as the input. This functionality is essential for robots that are tasked with everything from pursuing goals to stopping a ball, in the case of goalkeeper robots. It is equally crucial for autonomous vehicles to allow for high-level spatial reasoning and path planning. Similarly, it is useful in various human tracking systems, from those which try to understand customer behavior, as we saw in the case of retail, to those which constantly monitor football or basketball players during a game.

A relatively straightforward way to perform object tracking is to apply object detection to each image in a video sequence and then compare the instances of each object to determine how they moved. The drawback of this approach is that performing object detection for each individual image is typically expensive. An alternative approach would be to capture the object being tracked only once (as a rule, the first time it appears) and then discern the movements of that object without explicitly recognizing it in the following images. Finally, an object tracking method does not necessarily need to be capable of detecting objects; it can simply be based on motion criteria, without being aware that the object is being tracked.

How it works

As mentioned earlier in this guide, the goal of computer vision is to mimic the way the human visual system works. How is this achieved with algorithms? While this topic is too extensive to cover in a single article, you'll be introduced to the most important concepts here.

A general strategy

Deep learning methods and techniques have profoundly transformed computer vision, along with other areas of artificial intelligence, to such an extent that for many tasks its use is considered standard. In particular, Convolutional Neural Networks (CNN) have achieved beyond state-of-the-art results utilizing traditional computer vision techniques.

These four steps outline a general approach to building a computer vision model using CNNs:

1. Create a dataset comprised of annotated images or use an existing one. Annotations can be the image category (for a classification problem); pair's of bounding boxes and classes (for an object detection problem); or a pixel-wise segmentation of each object of interest present in an image (for an instance segmentation problem).

2. Extract, from each image, features pertinent to the task at hand. This is a key point in modeling the problem. For example, the features used to recognize faces, features based on facial criteria, are obviously not the same as those used to recognize tourist attractions or human organs.

3. Train a deep learning model based on the features isolated. Training means feeding the machine learning model many images and it will learn, based on those features, how to solve the task at hand.

4. Evaluate the model using images that weren't used in the training phase. By doing so, the accuracy of the training model can be tested.

This strategy is very basic but it serves the purpose well. Such an approach, known as supervised machine learning, requires a dataset that encompasses the phenomenon the model has to learn.

Existing datasets

Datasets are generally expensive to build, but they are critical for developing computer vision applications. Luckily, there are readily-available datasets. One of the most voluminous and well known is ImageNet, a dataset of 14 million images manually annotated using WordNet concepts. Within the global dataset, 1 million images contain bounding box annotations.

Another well-known one is the Microsoft Common Objects in Context (COCO), dataset, loaded with 328,000 images including 91 object types that would be easily recognizable by a 4-year-old, with a total of 2.5 million labeled instances.

While there isn't a plethora of available datasets, there are several suitable for different tasks, such as the CelebFaces Attributes Dataset (CelebA, a face attributes dataset with more than 200K celebrity images); the Indoor Scene Recognition dataset (15,620 images of indoor scenes); and the Plant Image Analysis dataset (1 million images of plants from 11 different species).

Training an object detection model

Viola and Jones approach

There are many ways to address object detection challenges. For years, the prevalent approach was one proposed by Paul Viola and Michael Jones in the paper, Robust Real-time Object Detection.

Although it can be trained to detect a diverse range of object classes, the approach was first motivated by the objective of face detection. It is so fast and straightforward that it was the algorithm implemented in point-and-shoot cameras, which allows for real-time face detection with little processing power.

The central feature of the approach is to train with a potentially large set of binary classifiers based on Haar features. These features represent edges and lines, and are extremely simple to compute when scanning an image.

Although quite basic, in the specific case of faces these features allow for the capturing of important elements such as the nose, mouth, or the distance between the eyebrows. It is a supervised method that requires many positive and negative examples of the type of object to be discerned.

This guide does not discuss the details of the algorithm because our focus is on deep learning methods. However, the video above shows a very interesting animation of how the algorithm detects Mona Lisa's face.

CNN-based approaches

Deep learning has been a real game changer in machine learning, especially in computer vision, where deep-learning-based approaches are now cutting edge for many of the usual tasks.

Among the different deep learning approaches proposed for accomplishing object detection, R-CNN (Regions with CNN features) is particularly simple to understand. The author's of this work propose a three-stage process:

1. Extract possible objects using a region proposal method.

2. Identify features in each region using a CNN.

3. Classify each region utilizing SVMs.

The region proposal method opted for in the original work was Selective Search, although the R-CNN algorithm is agnostic regarding the particular region proposal method adopted. Step 3 is very important as it decreases the number of object candidates, which makes the method less computationally expensive.

The features extracted here are less intuitive than the Haar features previously mentioned. To summarize, a CNN is used to extract a 4096-dimensional feature vector from each region proposal. Given the nature of the CNN, it is necessary that the input always have the same dimension. This is usually one of the CNN's weak points and the various approaches address this in different ways. With respect to the R-CNN approach, the trained CNN architecture requires inputs of a fixed area of 227 × 227 pixels. Since the proposed regions have sizes that differ from this, the authors' approach simply warps the images so that they fit the required dimension.

While it achieved great results, the training encountered several obstacles, and the approach was eventually outperformed by others. Some of those are reviewed in depth in the article, Object Detection with Deep Learning: The Definitive Guide.

Business use cases

Computer vision applications are increasingly employed by companies to answer business questions or to enhance their products. They are probably already a part of your everyday life, without you even noticing it. Following are some popular use cases.

Visual Search Engines

Visual search technology became available to the public with the appearance of Google Images back in 2001. A visual search engine is able to retrieve images that meet certain content criteria. Searching for keywords is a common use case, but sometimes we can present a source image and request that similar images be found. In certain cases, it is possible to specify more detailed search criteria, such as images of beaches, taken during the summer, containing at least ten people.

There are many visual search engines, either in the form of websites accessible directly or via an API, or in the form of mobile applications or their features.

The most well-known visual search websites are without a doubt Google Images, Bing, and Yahoo. For the first two, a set of keywords or an image can serve as the search input. The latter is known as a reverse image search. Yahoo allows search by keywords and the results are usually equally impressive, as you can see from the screenshot below.

There are other visual search sites that deserve attention, such as TinEye, focused exclusively on reverse image search, and Picsearch, which allows text searching only but has very broad coverage.

In the realm of mobile applications, offerings vary widely as visual search technology has been gradually incorporated as a standard feature.

There are implementations such as Google Goggles, later replaced by Google Lens, which can be used to obtain detailed information from images. For example, you can take a picture of your cat and get information about its breed, or if you are in a museum, the application can provide information about certain works of art.

In the e-commerce market, Pinterest offers Pinterest Lens. If you need outfit ideas inspired by your wardrobe (for example, you want to find new ways to wear your favorite jeans or blazer), you can take a photo of the item and Pinterest Lens will return outfit ideas that include compatible clothing items you can ultimately buy. Visual search for online shopping is one of the fastest growing trends from recent years.

Finally, a more advanced case of visual search is that of visual question-answering systems.

Face recognition at Facebook

Although photographic cameras capable of face detection for the purpose of performing auto focus have been around since the mid-2000s, yet more impressive results in facial recognition have been achieved in recent years. The most common (and controversial) application is perhaps to recognize a person in an image or video. This is especially so with security systems, but it also comes into play in social media when adding filters to faces, in photo management systems to be able to search by person, or even in preventing a person from voting more than once in an electoral process. Facial recognition can also be used in a more sophisticated way, such as to recognize emotions in facial expressions.

A use case that simultaneously aroused a lot of interest and concern is Facebook's facial recognition system. Some of the main objectives advanced by the development team were the possibility of protecting strangers from using photos in which a user appears (see example below), or informing people with a visual impairment who appears in a photo or video.

Beyond the worrisome aspects, this technology is very beneficial in multiple scenarios, including fighting cyber harassment.

Amazon Go

Tired of waiting in line at supermarkets and grocery stores? Amazon Go stores are an incredible experience. There are no lines or shipping boxes, all made possible thanks to the power of computer vision.

The idea is simple: Customer's enter the store, choose the products they want, and leave the store with them, without having to queue up to pay at the check-stand or self-check kiosk.

How is it possible? It functions thanks to a technology called Just Walk Out by Amazon.

Customers must download a mobile app that will help them identify themselves to Amazon and give them a QR Code that will allow them to enter Amazon Go stores. There are turnstiles at the store entrances through which customers have to pass, both to enter and leave the store in question. When entering, these turnstiles read the customer's QR Code. One nice feature is that customers can be accompanied by other people without the need for them to have the application installed.

Customers can move freely around the store. This is where computer vision comes into play. There is a series of sensors installed in the store, including cameras, motion sensors, and weight sensors in the items themselves. These devices gather info on what each person is doing. They detect the items that customers pick up from the shelves in real time. One can pick up an item and put it back later if they change their mind. However, the system ultimately charges the item to the first customer who picked it up, so if it is handed to another who wants it, the first will be financially responsible for it. A virtual shopping cart containing the items picked up is created and maintained in real time by the system. This makes the purchase process particularly pleasant.

When customers finish their shopping, they simply exit the store. When they pass through the turnstiles, the system – without asking the customers to scan the products or their QR Code – registers the sales and sends notifications to the customers to indicate that their confirmation is available.

Amazon Go is an example of how computer vision can have a positive impact on the real world and people's daily lives.

Tesla Autopilot

The idea that you can activate autopilot and ride along while your car does the driving is something more than a distant dream. Tesla's Autopilot technology provides autonomous driving features that are very convenient. It's not a completely autonomous system, as Uber's autonomous vehicles possess, but rather a sophisticated driving assistant that's authorized to drive the car on specific route segments. This is an important point that the company emphasizes: it is the driver's responsibility to control the vehicle under all circumstances.

The video above demonstrates Autopilot's capabilities. In the three external camera views located to the right of the main screen, computer vision implementations are visible. Autonomous driving is achieved with techniques like object detection and tracking.

For Autopilot to work, Tesla cars must be heavily equipped. Eight panoramic cameras give them 360° visibility at a range of 250 meters. Ultrasonic sensors have been installed to detect objects, as well as a radar that processes information about the surrounding environment. Thanks to all this, the cars are able to adjust their speed depending on traffic conditions, brake when approaching obstacles, maintain or change lanes, take a fork in the road, and park smoothly.

Tesla's Autopilot technology is another excellent example of the impressive impact computer vision has had on our most common daily activities.

In the healthcare sector, InnerEye by Microsoft is an incredibly valuable tool that assists radiologists, oncologists, and surgeons who work with radiology-based images. The primary goal of the tool is to accurately identify tumors among healthy anatomy in 3D images of cancerous growths.

Based on computer vision and machine learning techniques, the technology produces extremely detailed 3D modeling of tumors. The above screenshot shows a complete 3D segmentation of a brain tumor created by InnerEye. If you watch the whole video, you'll see that the expert controls the tool and guides it to perform the task, which means that InnerEye acts as an assistant.

In radiation therapy, for instance, InnerEye results make it possible to direct radiation specifically at the target tumor while preserving vital organs.

These results also help radiologists better understand sequences of images and whether a disease is progressing, stable, or reacting favorably to treatment, while taking into account the evolution of a tumor's size, among other things. In this way, medical imaging becomes a means of tracking and measuring.

Finally, InnerEye can be used to plan precision surgeries

I'm not Google, what now?

The fact that the computer vision implementations of large companies are the most often discussed does not mean that you have to be Google or Amazon to benefit from this machine learning technology. Businesses of all sizes can leverage their data with computer vision techniques in order to become more efficient and effective at what they do, all while making better decisions.

Let's examine the real-world experience of a smaller company:

We from Tryolabs helped a small risk management company based in San Francisco to build and implement a computer vision system able to scale image processing for roof inspections.

Before using computer vision, company's experts analyzed pictures taken by drones manually in order to detect damages on building roofs. Although the analysis was very precise, the service offered was not scalable due to time consuming nature and limited human resources.

To overcome this problem, we built a deep learning system able to understand images and automatically identify issues on roofs including water pooling, loose cables, and rust. To achieve this, we developed a deep neural network capable of detecting several issues in roof imagery, as well as a pipeline to analyze incoming images and an API to make the results accessible to external tools.

As a result, the company was able to increase order volume and revenue.

How to realize a computer vision project

Like with every innovation you consider worth pursuing in your organization, you should choose a strategic approach to implement a computer vision project.

A successful innovation with computer vision depends on your overall business strategy, your resources, and your data.

Here are some questions you can ask yourself, that should help you build the strategic roadmap of a computer vision project.

1. Should the computer vision solution reduce costs or increase revenue?

A successful computer vision project either reduces costs or increases revenue (or both) and you should define, which goal it is. Only this way will it have a major impact on your organization and its growth.

2. How are you going to measure the success of your computer vision project?

Each computer vision project is different and you need to define a success metric that makes sense for your specific project and which you'll be able to measure. Once that metric is set, you should make sure it is accepted by business people and data scientists alike.

3. Is the access to information guaranteed?

When starting computer vision initiatives, data scientists need to have easy access to information. They will need to work together with key people, possibly from different departments, such as the IT department for example. Those people need to support the project with business knowledge of some sorts and internal bureaucracy would be a main constraint.

4. Is your organization collecting the right data?

Computer vision algorithms are no magic. They need data to work, and they can only be as good as the data you feed in. There are different methods and sources to collect the right data, depending on your objectives. Anyhow, the more input data you have, the better the chances that your computer vision model will perform well. If you have doubts about the quantity and quality of your data, you can ask data scientists to help you evaluate the datasets and find the best way to get to third-party data, if necessary.

5. Is your organization collecting the data in the right format?

Besides having the right amount and type of data, you should also make sure you are collecting data in the right format. Imagine you have taken thousands of perfect pictures of smartphones (good resolution and white background) in order to train a computer vision model to detect them in images. Then you discover that it won't work because the actual use case was detecting people holding smartphones in various lighting/contrasts/backgrounds, and not the smartphones by themselves. Your past data collection effort would be nearly worthless, and you will need to start over. Also, you should understand if bias exists in the data being collected because algorithms will learn that bias.

The 5 Trends Dominating Computer Vision

Introduction

Research in computer vision has been booming over the past few years, thanks to advances in deep learning, increases in computing storage, and the explosion of big visual datasets. Every day, there are more computer vision applications in fields as diverse as autonomous vehicles, healthcare, retail, energy, linguistics, and more.

In this article, I'll present the 5 major trends that have dominated computer vision research in 2018. An exhaustive review is impossible, so I'll only share some of the accomplishments in the field that have most impressed me.

1 — Synthetic Data

Synthetic data has been a huge trend in computer vision researches this past year. They are data generated artificially to train deep learning models. For example, the SUNCG dataset is used for simulated indoor environments, the Cityscapes dataset is used for driving and navigation, and the SURREAL dataset of synthetic humans is used to learn pose estimation and tracking. Let's look at some of the best work utilizing synthetic data this year:

• In How Well Should You Label, the authors look at how coarsely the training labels must be to produce good segmentation quality from modern CNN architectures. This is important because synthetic data are usually known for their pixel-perfect quality. Performing their experiments on the Auto City dataset, the authors prove that the final segmentation quality is indeed strongly correlated with the amount of time spent labeling, but not so much with the quality of each individual label.

• Soccer on Your Tabletop presents a system that can take a video stream of a soccer game and transform it into a moving 3D reconstruction that can be projected onto a tabletop and viewed with augmented reality. The system extracts bounding boxes of the players, analyzes the human figures with pose and depth estimation models, and finally produces an astoundingly accurate 3D scene reconstruction.

• The human ability to simultaneously learn from various information sources is still lacking in most existing feature learning approaches. Cross-Domain Self-supervised Multi-task Feature Learning using synthetic imagery addresses this gap by proposing an original multi-task deep learning network that uses synthetic imagery to better learn visual representations in a cross-modal setting. Training the network through synthetic images dramatically reduces data annotations needed for multitask learning, which is costly and time-consuming. To bridge the cross-domain gap between real and synthetic data, adversarial learning is employed in an unsupervised feature-level domain adaptation method, which enhances performance upon the transfer of acquired visual feature knowledge to real-world tasks.

• Training Deep Networks with Synthetic Data proposes a refined approach for training deep neural network data for real object detection, relying on domain randomization of synthetic data. Domain randomization reduces the need for high-quality simulated datasets by intentionally and randomly disturbing the environment's textures to force the network to focus and identify the main features of the object. To augment the process's performance, additional training on real data in conjunction with synthetic data is performed, which bridges the reality gap, therefore yielding better performance results. Different approaches were proposed to exploit the potential of synthetic data, which suggests this area will further advance in the coming years.

2 — Visual Question Answering

Visual question answering (VQA) is a new and exciting problem that combines NLP and computer vision techniques. It typically involves showing an image to a computer and asking a question about that image that the computer must answer. The answer could be in any of the following forms: a word, a phrase, a Yes/No answer, multiple choice answers, or a fill-in-the-blank answer.

There have been various datasets developed recently to tackle this task, such as DAQUAR, Visual7W, COCO-QA, VQA. Let's look at some of the best models in question answering this year.

• Embodied QA reaches toward the goal of creating fully intelligent agents that can actively perceive, naturally communicate in an environment-grounded dialogue, and act and execute commands. Through goal-driven intelligent navigation of a 3D setting, the agent is asked to answer questions based on object recognition and visual grounding and understanding. Interestingly, the agent solely uses egocentric vision to navigate its surroundings. This means that the agent is not provided with a map and trained only via raw sensory inputs (pixels and words) and must rely on common sense in navigating an unfamiliar environment.

• Standard VQA models passively rely on large static datasets—unlike the interactive nature of human learning that's more sample efficient and less redundant. Learning by asking questions fills this research gap by introducing a more interactive VQA model that mimics natural learning. In this paper, the agent is trained to learn like a human by evaluating its prior acquired knowledge and asking good and relevant questions that maximize the learning signal from each image-question pair sent to the oracle. The paper also shows how interactive questioning significantly reduces redundancy and the required number of training samples to achieve accuracy increases of 40%.

• Inverse Visual QA (iVQA) joins the other models that aim to improve the performance of standard VQA models by focusing on developing visual grounding.

This paper inverses the popular VQA task so that the target is to generate a question given an image/answer pair. The learning biases of standard VQAs undermine the evaluation process. iVQA uses partially-generated questions with less biased learning priors corresponding to an image-answer pair to achieve more visual grounding.

• Interactive QA addresses one of the shortcomings of standard VQA models, which are mostly passive and do not train a fully intelligent agent capable of navigating, interacting, and performing tasks within its environment. The model uses a multi-level controller method with semantic spatial memory and collects a rich dataset of simulated realistic scenes and a wide range of questions to evaluate the model. It advances standard VQA towards the ultimate goal of creating fully visually intelligent agents.

• Effectively evaluating the performance of current state-of-the-art VQA models and preventing them from relying on biased training priors is an area that is still under development. To that end, the Grounded

Visual QA model offers a new method that directly dissociates the objects recognized from plausible prior answers, forcing the model to be more visually grounded. With the excellent results the paper has reported and the current community focus on this line of research, it's a promising sign for future innovative methods further advancing VQA models.

3 — Domain Adaptation

There are a couple of specific research directions that have been trending in 2018, and one is domain adaptation. This field is actually closely related to synthetic data. It tackles the big challenge of collecting labeled datasets for supervised learning and ensuring that the data are reliable and diverse enough. Essentially, how do we use one kind of data to prepare the network to cope with a different kind?

• Unsupervised Domain Adaptation with Similarity Learning deals with domain adaptation using adversarial networks. The author asks one network to extract features from a labeled source domain and another network to extract features from an unlabeled target domain, with similar but different data distribution. The classification in which the model is trained to discriminate the target prototype from all other prototypes is different. To label the image from the target domain, the author compares the embedding of an image with embeddings of prototype images from the source domain and then assigns the label of its nearest neighbors.

• Image to Image Translation for Domain Adaptation looks at domain adaptation for image segmentation, which is used widely in self-driving vehicles, medical imaging, and many other domains. Basically, domain adaptation techniques here must find a mapping structure from the source data distribution to the target data distribution. The approach uses 3 main techniques: (i) domain-agnostic feature extraction (the distributions of features extracted from both source and target domains are indistinguishable), (ii) domain-specific reconstruction (embeddings can be decoded back to the source and target domains), and (iii) cycle consistency (mappings are learned correctly).

• Conditional GAN for Structured Domain Adaptation offers a new method to overcome the challenges of cross-domain differences in semantic segmentation models with a structured domain adaptation method. Unlike unsupervised domain adaptation, the method does not assume the existence of cross-domain common feature space, and rather employs a conditional generator and a discriminator. Therefore, a conditional GAN is integrated into the CNN framework that transfers features of synthetic images to real-image like features. The method results outperform previous models, highlighting the growing potential of synthetic datasets in advancing vision tasks.

• Training deep learning-based models relies on large annotated datasets, which requires lots of resources. Despite achieving state-of-the-art performance in many visual recognition tasks, cross-domain differences still constitute a big challenge. To transfer knowledge across domains, Maximum Classifier Discrepancy for Unsupervised Domain Adaptation uses a novel adversarial learning method for domain adaptation without a need for any labeling information from the target domain. It's observed that minimizing the discrepancy between the probability estimates from two classifiers for samples from a target domain can produce class-discriminative features for various tasks, from classification to semantic segmentation.

4 — Generative Adversarial Networks

2018 has definitely been a big year for Generative Adversarial Networks (GAN), the most successful class of generative models for computer vision. Let's look at some of the best works that improve GAN models this year:

• Conditional GANs are already widely used for image modeling, but they are also very useful for style transfer. Particularly, they can learn salient features that correspond to specific image elements and then change them. In PairedCycleGAN for Makeup, the authors present a framework for makeup modification on photos. They train separate generators for different facial components and apply them separately, extracting facial components with a different network.

- Eye Image Synthesis with Generative Models looks at the problem of generating human eyes images. This is an interesting use case because we can use generated eyes to solve the gaze estimation problem — what is a person looking at? The authors use a probabilistic model of eye shape synthesis and a GAN architecture to generate eyes following that model.

- Generative Image In-painting with Contextual Attention looks at the challenging problem of filling in blanks on an image. Usually, we need to have an understanding of the underlying scene to do in-painting. This work instead uses a GAN model that can explicitly use features from the surrounding image to improve generation.

- Current state-of-the-art GAN-based text-to-image generation models encode textual descriptions only on the sentence level and overlook fine-grained information on the word-level that would improve the quality of generated images. AttnGAN proposes a novel word-level attention mechanism that's far more impressive in producing complex scenes.

- In contrast to the common belief that the success of neural networks mainly comes from their strong ability to learn from data, Deep Image Prior demonstrates the importance of the structure of the network for building good image priors. The paper proposes a decoder network as a prior for imaging tasks. Interestingly enough, the authors show that a generator network is adequate to capture a large amount of low-level image statistics prior to any learning. The authors also use the approach to investigate the information content retained at different levels of the network by producing so-called natural pre-images. Intriguingly, using the deep image prior as a regularizer, the pre-image obtained from even very deep layers still captures a large amount of information.

- Despite the success of GANs, no considerable success has been reported on the usage of their discriminator network as a universal loss function for common supervised tasks such as semantic segmentation. Matching Adversarial Networks highlights the reason behind this, namely that the loss function does not directly depend on the ground truth labels during generator training, which leads to random production of samples from data distributions without correlating the input-output relations in a supervised fashion. To overcome this, the paper proposes replacing the discriminator with a matching network—while taking into account both the ground truth outputs as well as the generated examples—which is facilitated by a Siamese network architecture.

5 — 3D Object Understanding

3D object understanding is critical for deep learning systems to successfully interpret and navigate the real world. For instance, a network may be able to locate a car in a street image, color all of its pixels, and classify it as a car. But does it fully understand where the car in the image is, with respect to other objects in the street?

The work in 3D object understanding spans a wide variety of research areas including object detection, object tracking, pose estimation, depth estimation, scene reconstruction, and more. Let's cover major papers in this field in 2018:

• Detect-and-Track is an extension of Mask R-CNN, one of the most promising approaches to image segmentation that appeared back in 2017. The authors propose a 3D Mask R-CNN architecture that uses spatiotemporal convolutions to extract features and recognize poses directly on short clips. The complete architecture can be seen below. It achieves state-of-the-art results in pose estimation and human tracking.

• Pose-Sensitive Embeddings for Person Re-Identification tackles the challenge of person re-identification. Usually, this problem is solved with retrieval-based methods that derive proximity measures between the query image and stored images from some embedding space. The paper instead proposes a novel way to incorporate information about the pose directly into the embedding and improve re-identification results. You can see the architecture below.

• 3D Poses from a Single Image presents a very surprising approach to pose estimation. It generates the 3D mesh of a human body directly through an end-to-end convolutional architecture that combines pose estimation, segmentation of human silhouettes, and mesh generation. The key insight is that it uses SMPL, a statistical body shape model that provides a good prior for the human body's shape. Consequently, it manages to construct a 3D mesh of a human body from a single-color image.

• Flow Track deals with the problem of object tracking. It's an extension of discriminative correlation filters, which learn a filter that corresponds to the object and apply it to all video frames. The model architecture has a spatial-temporal attention mechanism that attends across different time frames in the video.

• Just like Flow Track described above, Correlation Tracking also deals with object tracking and also uses correlation filters. However, it doesn't use a deep neural network; instead, it has reliability information — meaning that the authors add a term to the objective function that models how reliable the learned filter is.

We hope you enjoyed the reading and that this introductory guide helped you gain a better understanding of what computer

vision is all about, how it works, and how it
is applied in the real-world.

www.ingramcontent.com/pod-product-compliance
Lightning Source LLC
Chambersburg PA
CBHW052239150726
48002CB00003B/1498